ORCHID

T0414319

LIFE CYCLES

Words that look like **this** can be found in the glossary on page 24.

BookLife
PUBLISHING

©2021
BookLife Publishing Ltd.
King's Lynn
Norfolk PE30 4LS

A catalogue record for this book is available from the British Library.

ISBN: 978-1-83927-158-8

Written by:
Brenda McHale

Edited by:
Shalini Vallepur

Designed by:
Danielle Webster-Jones

CONTENTS

LIFE CYCLES

WHAT IS A LIFE CYCLE?

All animals, plants and humans go through different stages of their life as they grow and change. This is called a life cycle.

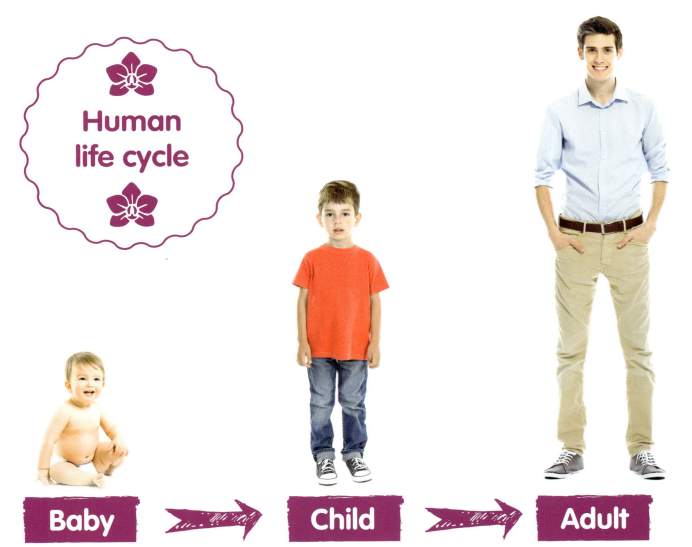

Human life cycle

Baby → Child → Adult

WHAT IS AN ORCHID?

An orchid is a type of plant that produces flowers. There are more than 22,000 **species**. Some grow in soil and some grow on trees or rocks.

These orchids are being grown in pots.

SEEDS

Each plant makes thousands of very tiny seeds. They usually grow in pods, like peas. Inside the seed is the **embryo** that will grow into the orchid plant.

These seed pods are full of tiny white seeds.

The pod splits and the light seeds get blown by the wind.
Only a few seeds from each pod will grow into a new plant.

They blow in the wind like these dandelion seeds.

SEEDLINGS

The seed splits and starts to grow into a seedling. A root grows from the seed into soil or the bark of a tree and takes in **nutrients** and water.

These seedlings are being grown to sell.

These orchid seedlings are growing on a tree.

Soon, small leaves grow. The leaves use sunlight to make food and help the plant get bigger.

PLANTS

Orchid plants that grow on trees or rocks have lots of roots. These roots collect water from the air and help the orchid plant to stay in place.

Roots

Sometimes, the roots hang down like a beard.

The leaves can be different shapes. Some are long and thin but others are round. The leaves might be waxy if they grow somewhere dry.

Long waxy leaves

FLOWERS

Some orchids have tiny flowers smaller than a grain of rice. Other flowers are bigger than a hand. Many orchids have a special petal called a lip that insects stand on to collect **nectar**.

This butterfly is sitting on the lip.

Pollen gets stuck to insects when they come to collect nectar. They carry this pollen to other orchids. This is called pollination. These orchids will use the pollen to make new seeds.

This bee is collecting nectar.

ORCHIDS

Orchids grow outdoors but people like to keep them as house plants. They are colourful and beautiful.

Orchid flowers usually last for around eight weeks before dropping off. The plant can flower again every year if it is healthy.

TYPES OF ORCHID

Some orchid petals look like other things. One plant is called the monkey orchid – can you see why?

It's easy to see why it gets its name but no one knows why it looks like a monkey.

One species is called the fly orchid. This has a lip shaped like a fly. This helps to **attract** other flies to pollinate the plant.

Do you think fly orchids are beautiful?

ORCHID FACTS

Vanilla comes from orchid seeds. We use vanilla to flavour cakes, ice cream and many other foods.

Dried vanilla pods

Like insects, some birds also enjoy orchids. Hummingbirds use their long beaks and tongues to reach the nectar in the orchid flower.

WORLD RECORD BREAKERS

Oldest Orchid

Scientists found an insect trapped in **amber** that had orchid pollen on its leg. The amber is over 45 million years old.

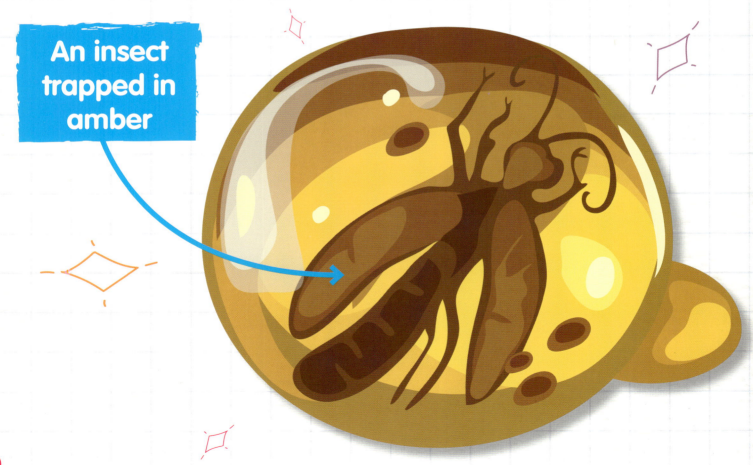

An insect trapped in amber

The Ghost Orchid

Britain's **rarest** flower is the ghost orchid. Scientists thought it was **extinct** but a single plant was found in 2016. Spooky!

LIFE CYCLE OF AN ORCHID

1 The seed splits and grows a root and sprouts new leaves.

2 The sprouting plant grows into a plant with flowers.

LIFE CYCLES

4 New seeds grow.

3 Insects pollinate the flowers.

GET EXPLORING!

Why not find pictures of orchids and draw or paint them?
You could even find a real one in a flower shop to copy.

GLOSSARY

amber a hard, yellow material from the resin of very old trees

attract to pull towards

embryo the part of a plant's seed that grows into a plant

extinct when an animal or plant no longer exists

nectar a sweet liquid made by plants

nutrients natural things that plants and animals need in order to grow and stay healthy

pollen powder that is made by the flowers on a plant

rarest the hardest to find of its kind

species groups of very similar animals or plants that can create young together

INDEX

PHOTO CREDITS

All images are courtesy of Shutterstock.com, unless otherwise specified. With thanks to Getty Images, Thinkstock Photo and iStockphoto. Front cover & 1 – My Sunnyday. 2 – Huy Thoai. 3 – TheAlphaWolf [CC BY-SA 3.0 (https://creativecommons.org/licenses/by-sa/3.0)], ForGaby, Nattavut. 4 – pikselstock, 5 second Studio, Inara Prusakova, Matagonca. 5 – InspiringMoments. 6 – Peter Krisch. 7 – Biehler Michael, Peter Krisch, Bettina Calder. 8 – Pengejar Senja. 9 – Davdeka. 10 – kamomeen. 11 – Lesar Unat Basukala. 12 – Angela N Perryman. 13 – Sergei Bolshakov. 14 – New Africa. 15 – gata_iris. 16 – cotosa, tratong. 17 – COULANGES. 18 – Elena Veselova, Natalia van D. 19 – Sue Bishop. 20 – lady-luck. 21 – jakk wong, Aniko Gerendi Enderle, Fotomay. 22 – Pengejar Senja, Edward Fielding, Lukas Budinsky, Liz Grogan. 23 – Zayakina Yuliya.